"Totally C

Contents

Prologue

Part 1: Stimulus

Part 2: Exploration

Part 3: Plays & Sketches

Part 4: Reprise

Prologue

"Totally obliviated ..."

The three men standing in a group had just come out from a pub. They were parting to go back to work, and one was describing a scene from the previous night: "... and there he was, totally obliviated". The others nodded wisely.

I walked on a few paces, then stopped.

"Totally obliviated ..."

The more I thought about it, the more I wondered. What did he mean? - Drunk? Forgotten? Dead? .... But what an expressive word!

In this book I hope you'll find pleasure in looking at the world through my quirky eyes. Nothing is ever as dull as it seems, and life is too serious to be taken too seriously.

Otherwise you too might end up totally obliviated!

Part 1: Stimulus

I'd never been on a walking holiday before, and I'd never been to the Lake District either. So when we put ourselves down for a week of both one summer, it was a double first for me.

I associated the lakes with rain and mist, and walking was something done reluctantly behind the dogs. Imagine my surprise when I found blue cloudless skies and a real pleasure in scrambling up scree and round boulders for that distant view of the Isle of Man.

But the real reason for being there was for the 'special interest' sessions in the evening. While taking the weight off the blistered feet, I was going to learn the art of creative writing. And all in a week.

Whether I succeeded, dear reader, you must judge for yourself!

On the first evening, we were asked to write about something we'd picked up during the day. Apart from sunstroke that is. I'd found a small piece of bone, and went on the defensive straight away ...

Only a Bone

It's not so much I don't know what to say, it's just .... No, let's be honest - it's entirely that I don't know what to say. I've not the first idea in my mind of anything interesting, useful, or entertaining to say about this piece of bone.

"Why pick it up in the first place then?", I hear you ask. Good question. There I was at a quarter to eight this morning, wandering up the hillside taking the pre-breakfast air, and there was this piece of bone. Actually I was looking for something completely different - a round pebble among the sharp scree, an orchid in the gorse, a yeti track in the bog, or anything - but no luck. Only a bone I bring you, and a dry bone at that.

So, what about the bone?
Whose bone? Sheep's bone?
One who never made it home?
Left to meet its fate alone?
Poor old thing, and was it worry
from a dog that made him hurry
down the slope, to slip and slide
and end up dead? That's agnicide!
And also pure conjecture too.

What else to say? There's Yorick, who
was dug up by the Bard, "Alas
poor Yorick" - was it Fortinbras
who said it, or the smoking prince?
Whichever, it's no matter, since
the thing they spoke of was a skull
and this is not, it's far more dull.
In fact so dull, I think I'll wrap up,
cease, desist and shut my trap up.
Thank you all for having ears.
(Sits down amid the thunderous cheers!)

During the week, as a loosener, we were asked to invent an alphabetical sentence. How about this?

Kenyan Copy

A Beautiful, Coy Damsel Entered Fearfully, Giving Her Instructions: "Just Kill Lions; Monochrome; Nairobi Original Pictures". Quizzically, Richard Understood: "Vera Will Xerox Your Zebras".

The other amusing exercise was to try our hand at a 'mini-saga' or two. These are supposed to have a proper beginning, middle and end, and be <u>exactly</u> fifty words long. Naturally, I cheated ...

A bientôt Dieppe

Oh oui, pour moi la France est belle,
Son vin, ses plages, sa vie;
Vacances passées en plein soleil
Sont all too soon finies;
Le car ferry à Newhaven
Is waiting at the quai,
And now we're there en Angleterre
There's nothing left to say -
- Yer know what I mean?

And in a slightly more conformist vein ...

Publishers be Damned

"Catch us a fish", they said. So I caught them a fish, a whale of a fish I thought.
I waited; and after a week I began to worry.
Then the telegram arrived: "Margaret Thatcher has today agreed rights to her autobiography with ... ".
I read no more - we had lost!

*When asked to write something on the subject of either 'Sunset',
'A day by the Sea', or 'Exploring the Universe', I was tempted
to try to include all three in one offering. In the event I hadn't
explored much of the universe by the time the supper bell rang,
so you're spared the full effect ...*

Daily Love

My love creeps early to my room
and wakes me with a gentle kiss.
I rise, and slowly, bit by bit,
expose my night-white body to her gaze.
Stretching, shaking off my clinging sloth
I greet her - for at night she is not there.
Ablutions done, I hurry down
to meet her now before the kitchen window,
and breakfast gladly in her cheerful sight.
What shall we do together this fine day,
my love and I?

Decision made, a picnic packed,
we take the train towards the distant shore.
Surf, shells and sand seem sympathetic
to my loved one's glance. The day moves on and,
as is natural for one with her hot passions,
she hourly now begins to lose her midday glow;
begins to dip towards the west horizon:
a quarter gone, then half, then - stately, slow,
the earth's diurnal movement
parts her from my sight;
a last brief smile,
and then my love,
Goodnight!

Part 2: Exploration

What's a week in Wordsworth's world worth?
Well, read on.

When I got home, I decided that I'd try to keep the momentum of the week going and write something, however little, each day. This part of the book shows some of the results.

When you start looking for subjects to write about, you suddenly find you're seeing things you may otherwise never have noticed. I'm told the same thing happens if you take up painting or drawing. Here's two examples I found in one day.

Scene in the Garden

Yesterday the local black ants evicted their winged brothers from the nest with a bluster of activity. We'd never seen it before - do they do it each year? Always at the end of July?

The poor unfortunates rose like dusty smoke from their home to head - who knows where? To east, to west? - no way seemed best. Are these the drones of the ant world? Their task fulfilled, now forcibly freed to ride the wind to oblivion?

***

The vine sends out its grasping shoots,
Two feet, even three feet long.
Where does it get its water from?
There's been no rain to speak of now
For several weeks, and yet somehow
These tender tendrils grow with grace
And stretch across each open space.

A waving wall of growing green.

I've always had a soft spot for August. I think it's because it was the only month in the whole year when you knew you didn't have to go to school. So when the first of the month dawned as cloudless as could be, I decided it deserved a dedication.

August 1st

Today is the first day of August.

Not a cloud in the sky and the temperature's high,
in the nineties they say.

Not a day for much work.

I made Chiswick by ten, had a meeting, and then
changed my plans for the day.

Instead of a tube to the centre of town,
I drove my car home,
had a drink and
cooled down.

The telephone may have its drawbacks,

But at least you can sit with an iced gin and it
and do business that way.

It was a beautiful summer, and I found it easier to keep my literary ideas flowing in the lazy, hazy days than I did later in the year when the nights drew in and the brain grew soggy. Here's another one from the heatwave.

Thoughts beneath a Rhododendron Tree

There's something quite odd about ...
sitting in the evening air
in shorts, your legs and shoulders bare,
with cloudless sky and setting sun
soon disappearing, dinner done
and coffee coming - when you feel
a drop of moisture, sharp as steel.

It makes you start, you look about,
what joker's playing tricks? The lout,
I'll get him! But you look again
and find that no-one's there. Explain
that if you can!

        Ah well, you see
beneath this rhododendron tree
you get a sort of sticky spray,
as if the leaves are sweating. Say
you leave a table or a chair
below it, you'll soon notice where
they've gone all tacky. So that's why
it seems to rain when all is dry.

Wasps

"You've got another wasps nest!"

Emma had been staying with us for a few days and, exploring parts of the garden which we stay-at-homes never visit, she found a wasps nest in an old post hole. Some animal had broken into the top and exposed the inside, but it was still a live nest for all that, with wasps winging their way in and out of the underground remains.

Seeing it there reminded me of other wasp adventures we'd had. I remember once they tried a cheeky intrusion into our bedroom.

Spots of grey started to appear on the ceiling one summer, and I immediately thought it was a spreading fungus - the house had had a history of dry rot. But lying in bed on a Sunday morning I saw a wasp fly in through the open window, head straight for the biggest of the spots, and start to work its way diligently round the edge.

It was building a nest, right there in full view on the bedroom ceiling! The other spots, it seemed, were failed first starts. Fascinated, we let it carry on for a few days, and soon the spot had grown to resemble a small upturned egg-cup. At this we felt enough was enough, and kept the window closed to put a stop to it.

Presumably the poor wasp had to start again somewhere else - we were left with a small paper egg-cup as a souvenir.

Each evening, if I have time, I make a note of things that have caught my attention during the day. Often nothing happens to them, but occasionally something will interest me enough to turn itself into a page of prose. The one below came from a day when I ended up thoroughly lost in the suburbs of South London.

Directed by Dishes

Once upon a time I was taught to tell north from south without using a compass or the sun or the stars. "Look at a tree in a wood", I was told, "and see which side has moss on it". Assuming of course that you could find a tree, the side with moss on was supposed to face north, away from the sun.

I'll admit I've never had to put this useful piece of information to the test. But it strikes me that nowadays there's another way to tell direction, and one which is likely to be more useful in urban areas where there are not many moss covered trees to be seen.

I refer of course to the spreading satellite dishes.

These baleful ears all point in the same direction, listening for a faint signal from the man made moon in the sky which, due to geometry and Newtonian physics, is vaguely towards the south.

So moss to the north or ears to the south, the choice is yours.

Or you could just buy a compass.

Baker's Doesn't

Seen on a baker's van in a market town:

"High on quality, Low on price"

But when he opened his sliding door, he covered up the middle part of the message, and it became simply:

"High on price"!!

I wonder if he ever noticed.

Lean and Rich

I had to take my car in for servicing the other day, and was told it was 'running too rich' and they'd adjusted it to run 'leaner'.

I must confess I'd never really thought of lean as being the opposite of rich before - after all you can get thin millionaires can't you?

Doing IT

Seen in the car window of a consultant in Information Technology:

> Jockeys take a fence to do it
> Campers sleep in tents to do it
> Sailors do it on the sea
> But I just do I.T.

And finally, a modern ballad of our times. The clue to the title is hidden in the song.

WYGNAWYS

Take your floppy out of me before we warm start,
Make sure your RAM is checked for all corruption,
Then activate your dongle to ensure that we're secure,
We mustn't risk another interruption,

Execute your program to manipulate my cells,
And open up your spread-sheet in my core,
Then tap your input in, and let the run begin,
And only stop me when you've got no more.

Resulting from this action, multiplication and subtraction
Then division in my cells will soon appear,
And in a little while we'll create an output file,
The results of your endeavours are beginning to come
clear,

You can check it as it grows, but as everybody knows
Now what you get's not always what you see,
When the output comes out <u>so,</u>
You'll want to have another go
And run another set of data through me.

Part 3: Plays & Sketches

Living in a village community gives lots of opportunities to write odd plays and sketches: for the bowls club, the historical society, the twinning association, etc, etc. "In jokes" form an essential part of this sort of presentation, but the ones that follow stand largely on their own two feet.

The Hindsight Saga

The local amateur dramatic society wanted to do "a play in a day" for charity. This needed a basic script to be written before the event, which would then be cast and mutilated as necessary on the day.

We came up with the idea of running a series of scenes from different periods in history, starting with Shakespearian times and ending at the present day. It was to follow the fortunes of a particular family, and inevitably became known as "The Hindsight Saga".

In total it ran for 50 pages; this is the start of the Shakespearian scene, as Horatio Hindsight is given some bad news by his mother.

***

Mother   Alas, the Hindsight curse has struck again!
Horatio, thy father lies bereft of life,
As did the parrot in the Python sketch.

Horatio   What means this, mother?

Mother   These two things, my son.
First, from this stage we must remove his corpse.

Horatio   Why so?

Mother   To keep the cast from tripping over him.

(They remove the corpse with much business)

Horatio	The second thing?
Mother	A sudden greatness, Thrust upon thy young and noble shoulders, Hast gained thee now the title Baron Hindsight; And thou shouldst know the bloody violent curse Attending on all men who bear that name.
Horatio	What curse is this?
Mother	A deadly curse That kills thee *(acts)* just like that!
Horatio	And none escape it?
Mother	None that we're aware of.

(Enter an Old Retainer carrying a framed picture of the recently deceased Baron. He goes to replace the one already hanging on the wall)

Mother	Each time we change the picture on the wall, To show the face of he who went before.

(Business of them all helping to swap the pictures. Exit Mother at end of business)

Horatio	How came this curse to be?
Old Ret	I'll tell thee that, young master. A tale as old as time itself, And half as old as me.

(Horatio does some mental calculations)

Horatio	Thou art twice as old as time?
Old Ret	*(Who's a bit deaf, looks at his timepiece)* A quarter after eight.
Horatio	No matter, tell thy tale.

Old Ret	It's very long.
Horatio	Then cut it short, If possible without inflicting pain.
Old Ret	Well once there lived in olden days a witch, A wily witch with wooden besom too ... *(Business as Horatio misunderstands 'besom')* ... The Hindsights of the day ran foul of her, I don't know why or how, but since that day This curse has come to haunt the next in line.
Horatio	And now 'tis me!
Old Ret	'Tis right, alas I see, Be thou as chaste as ice, as pure as snow, Thou can'st not now escape thy due calamity. *(Exits)*

***

And so it went on.

And on.

And on.

But we collected nearly £1,000 for charity.

Pantomimes

I've written a few pantomimes for the same society, and tend to work to a regular format, which I explained in the following Producer's Notes to 'Cinderella'.

***

This pantomime uses three different full sets, separated by half set or front of curtain scenes to allow for backstage activity.

A list of songs is included for your guidance. Where special words have been written (eg. for the inevitable "Sisters"), these are also included. But use your imagination and feel free to put in whatever seems to fit, or whatever your pianist and performers can handle!

The concept of the Community Song is probably familiar to you, when the audience is invited to come up on the stage to help out, and some sort of raucous competition ensues between those brave enough to come up and those left behind sitting in the auditorium. The positioning of this event just before the final scene also gives any cast members not involved plenty of time to change into their finery for the Walkdown.

I use the general convention that immortals speak in rhyme and mortals in prose; *"In Pantomimes that's how it goes"*, says Gloria. Of course this leads to interesting problems if mortals and immortals speak to each other, as when Cinders meets the Fairy Godmother in disguise. I hope I have resolved this reasonably successfully. You will also see Griselda slipping from mortality to immortality as Gloria's potion starts to work!

So good luck with your show. Put in local variations as you wish, and if you think you can improve on the verse then do that too! Have fun - otherwise, why do it?

21

To show what I mean about the prose/verse combination, here is an extract from the first meeting between Cinders and the disguised Fairy Godmother (FG).

***

FG   I'm very grateful, what's your name
              girl?

Cind.   Cinderella.

FG   *(To herself)*   What a shame!

Cind.   I beg you pardon?

FG   Nothing dear.
              I think I knew your mother. Queer
              how these things happen.

Cind.   I don't follow!

FG   Never mind, I mustn't wallow!
              Come on, let's get there before
              the shops close. *(They start to walk off)*
                    I can see that you're
              the very image of you mother!

Cind.   Really?

FG   *(Musing)*   Yes, but that's another
              story - full of hearts and breaks.
              (Suddenly)
              Come on, let's buy these tarts and cakes!

Cind.   What sort of cakes?

FG   I have a feeling
              I'd find fairy cakes appealing!

(Exit Cinders with FG on their way to the town)

*And another example from the same pantomime - where Gloria,
the bad but incompetent fairy, is trying to mix a magic potion to
make Griselda, the wicked Stepmother, immortal.*

The test, of course, is to see if Gloria starts to speak in rhyme!

***

Gloria   Oh please Miss, give me one more go
to get it right!

Gris.   The answer's NO!

Gloria   Hang on, you just spoke that in rhyme!
Perhaps it's worked!

Gris.   I haven't time
to argue with the likes of you,
I've got much better things to do.
Pack up your pot and go to grass!
You've failed!
(To audience) This Pantomime's a farce!
How can you get your money's worth
with fools like that? Just how on earth
am I supposed to be the scary
villain when <u>she's</u> more like Mary
Poppins than a wicked fairy?
(Pause)
I think that smoke got to my head!
Let's start the show again instead.

(Exits)

And from 'Robin Hood' this time, we find Queen Fay of the Forest Fairies about to confront two of the Merry Men.

***

Fairy 1   Have you heard the news my lady?

Fairy 2   Robin Hood's to leave the shady
Forest for a life more formal.

Fairy 3   Mortals seem to think that's normal!

Q. Fay   Yes my elves, the news is good,
And not the least for Robin Hood;
Now Nottingham's restored to peace
He's marrying the Sheriff's niece.

Fairy 4   <u>Mar</u>rying?

Q. Fay   A mortal custom.

Fairy 5   What's it mean?

Fairy 6   I wouldn't trust 'em!

Q. Fay   Marrying is when they see
That sometimes one and one make three!

Fairy 7   One and one make three? How so?

Q. Fay   I'll tell you later Moth. Now go
And let the other fairies hear
The news you have. It's sure to cheer
Them up a bit -
(Fairies exit) - oh dearie me!
It must be time for fairy tea!
But, just a minute, who comes near?
What hempen homespuns have we here?

(Little John and Much Binding enter with bows and arrows)

Q. Fay   It's Little John and that Much Binding!
          Now then you two, you be minding
          What you do in this here wood,
          I'd say you mean to do no good!

L.John   Who's that?

Much B.   A fairy!

L.John   I'll be jiggered!

Much B. *(To L.John)* Don't say why we've come!

Q. Fay   I've figured!
          Could it be to hunt for deer?
          They say that there's a few round here.

          (They try to hide their bows)

L.John   Us hunt for deer?

Much B.   Say that again?

Q. Fay   Why hide the bows? It's very plain
          You've come to catch a hind or two
          To serve at Robin's banquet - true?

L.John   Well, put like that ...

Much B.   ... What can we say?

Q. Fay   Not much, Much. Now, hear what I say,
          You'll leave the rabbits, deer and birds
          To live in peace here. Violent words
          And violent deeds are not much cared for
          In my forest. We're prepared for
          Folk like you to come along,
          That's why we're going to sing this song!

                    ***

At which they are lead into the Community Song!

There's Poetry in Pantomime

There's poetry in Pantomime -
I don't just mean in speaking rhyme,
But hidden in the storyline as well;
The characters are comical
In matters anatomical,
But strike a balance in the tale they tell.

>The baddies enter downstage left,
>And give the kids a fright;
>But then the fairy calms them down
>By entering stage right.

There's poetry in Pantomime -
I guess it's been there all the time
From origins in street-performing mummers:
"Oh no you won't! - Oh yes I will!"
This age-old formula is still
The best to get involvement from all comers.

>Will you help us sing this song?
>Then come up on the stage -
>And bring your granny if you like,
>We take them any age!

There's poetry in Pantomime -
Its study forms a paradigm
Of all the daily struggles still occurring;
It's timeless, but it's up to date,
It's pageant, yet it's intimate
And deals with themes both delicate and stirring.

So when you see your local Am Dram
Putting on a show,
Don't think it's not your scene,
Just leave your TV off and go,   *(please, please!)*
You may not quite believe it now,
But afterwards you'll know -

>There's poetry in Pantomime!

Marzipal

Away from the pantomimes, I wrote a play about Megabux, a multi-national chemical company which mistakenly released news of a product it didn't have. The product 'Marzipal', dreamed up for a computer training course, promised to be a sure cure for all ailments. The stock market reacted enthusiastically, leaving the Managing Director with a problem.

We join the play just as salvation seems to be at hand. Herr Schuppenhauer from Austria claims to have actually invented such a product, and has come to sue Megabux for breach of patent. But he doesn't know they don't have a product - and they don't want him to know - so delicate negotiations are in hand, and Bruce Robinson and Clare Simpson of Megabux are walking on the proverbial thin ice.

***

Herr S   *(To Bruce)* So, it is you that has taken over my product!

Bruce   Not precisely.

Clare   We didn't know about your product, Herr Schuppenhauer.

Herr S   Not know about it? But your press release in great detail described my product.

Clare   Not <u>your</u> product.

Herr S   Yes, my product. *(Pats his case)* I have papers here to prove it. I show you ... *(He begins to open the case)*

Bruce   It may sound very similar, but believe me we knew nothing about what you were doing.

Herr S   You are expecting me to believe that two independent people can come up with exactly this same idea at the same time?

27

Clare	Apparently, yes.
Bruce	It has happened before you know, two people coming up with the same invention at the same time.
Herr S	I do not believe it. This is some plan of yours to rob me of my title.
Clare	No, Herr Schuppenhauer, it's not like that.
Herr S	Your company, already fat with profits from other peoples' work, found out about my discovery and decided to steal it.
Bruce	Listen, Herr Schuppenhauer ...
Herr S	Steal it from me by pretending to have found it first! By using the vast machinery of Megabux Chemicals to tell the world of your wonderful new product, and giving it a different name.
Clare	Herr Schupp ...
Herr S	No doubt you have concocted much back-up material, showing how and when it was discovered, by whom and where. No doubt you will have gone to the trouble of registering it, and have all your own paperwork ready to prove your claim to it. No doubt you think that because I am a little man from a little town in a little country, I will not put up a fight against you, the giant multinational mogul.
Bruce	Look, you don't quite understand ...
Herr S	Oh I understand. I understand only too well. I know how big companies like yours get rich. I know how you scan the world for other people's ideas, and then when you see one which

looks like it might make somebody a profit, you *obtain* the details and set up your own pack of laboratory hounds on the trail.

Clare   I think your jumping to the wrong conclusion here, Herr Schupp ...

Herr S   Oh no. I know how companies like yours operate. I am not just off a banana boat you know.

Bruce   But in this case you're wrong. May we explain our position?

Herr S   Ah yes. This is where I sit back and listen to the presentation of the facts of the matter as compiled by the corporate moles of Megabux Chemicals. Where is the audio-visual display, the dim lights, the soft music? Perhaps a cigar and a brandy to put me in a receptive mood?

Clare   Herr Schuppenhauer, we should make one thing plain. We don't have a product.

(There is a pause while this sinks in)

Herr S   You don't have a product?

Bruce   Marzipal doesn't exist. It never existed. It's a figment of our imagination.

Herr S   You, Megabux Chemicals, declare to the whole world you have a miracle cure for all these problems, and - it doesn't exist?

Clare   I'm afraid so.

Herr S   Is this some new trick in the international business game that I have not met before?

Bruce   No trick, Herr Schuppenhauer, I'm afraid it was a mistake.

Herr S	A mistake. You expect me to believe this?
Clare	Even companies like Megabux Chemicals can make a mistake from time to time.
Herr S	Oh come now! An error of judgement, an ill-advised decision, perhaps I could believe - but this? Launching a product that you don't even have onto the international market place? By mistake? No, you will have to pull the other one!
Bruce	Unfortunately it's true.
Herr S	You are being serious!
Clare	Deadly and in earnest.
Herr S	You have no product!

(Clare and Bruce shake their heads)

Bruce	And so we weren't out to rob you of your royalties after all.
Herr S	I see. *(Looks pensive)* This changes the ball-game, nicht wa? You have no product. I see.
Clare	In fact we were rather hoping ...
Herr S	*(Chuckling to himself)* No product!
Clare	... rather hoping that we could negotiate with you for the rights to use yours.
Herr S	*(Brightly)* My dear Miss Simpson! That is an entirely different matter. You wish to enter into a, how do you say it, *business arrangement* with me!

***

But things don't quite turn out that way. Go and see the play to find out why!

30

Part 4: Reprise

Reprise - an act of retaliation: recapture: compensation.

Not a retaliation I hope: perhaps a recapture of your interest and a compensation if drama wasn't your scene.

Must a sonnet always be about love, the universe and everything? Obviously not!

Autumn Burn-up

I burnt the boxes - took the jumbled pile
In three short journeys to the leaf-strewn patch,
Set out the smallest, stuffed with paper, while
I fumbled in my pocket for a match.

This summer was so hot and dry, remember
How noses peeled, unwatered grass turned brown?
Too risky then, I waited till November
Before I made a move to bring them down.

And leaving it so long it's just my luck,
Sure autumn mists encroaching in the night
Have seeped the cardboard's hydrophilic struc-
ture; that's to say, the damp things wouldn't light!

So cheating, I went back inside the shed
And brought some kindling wood outside instead.

Hey! If I can do a Sonnet, perhaps I can do something more difficult, like those French forms I've read about. Let's have a go at a Rondeau.

The Taming of the Sheep

And so to bed, it's getting late,
I'm tired and I can hardly wait
    To slide inside the linen sack
    And stretching lengthways on my back
Attain that somnolescent state

That lasts for seven hours, or eight,
To sleep, perchance to dream of Kate
    And tame the Shrew with one great whack,
    And so to bed.

But if I find that it's my fate
To stay awake, I'll contemplate
    Those members of the woolly pack
    Where some are white and some are black,
I'll count the sheep that jump the gate,
    And so to bed.

I find this is rather like painting by numbers! Let's try a Triolet or two.

Glove Match

There never was another,
    We were made to be a pair;
No father and no mother,
There never was another
Whose affections I could smother,
    For a glover made us, brother.
There never was another,
    We were made to be a pair.

The Proverbial Bird

A bird in the hand
    Is worth two in the bush,
It is quite simply grand,
A bird in the hand,
But you must understand
    That this bird is no thrush!
A bird in the hand
    Is worth two in the bush.

"The Villanelle is a difficult form to construct in English, because English has so few rhyming words". Really? Let's see what we can do.

Eddie's Caff

When you decide to stop and eat
      While shopping on a rainy day,
Choose Eddie's caff in Seaton Street.

Come on in and take a seat,
      The atmosphere is light and gay
When you decide to stop and eat.

If you've got some friends to meet,
      Say, Auntie Kay or Uncle Ray,
Choose Eddie's caff in Seaton Street.

Just take a break and rest your feet,
      I'll guarantee you'll want to stay,
When you decide to stop and eat.

Famous faces, the elite,
      They wouldn't hesitate to say,
"Choose Eddie's caff in Seaton Street".

Starter, entree and a sweet
Are always worth the price you pay;
When you decide to stop and eat,
Choose Eddie's caff in Seaton Street.

And now for the Haiku -

Economhaikul

A means of saying
Universal truths in short
Saves us energy.

Pet Problems

Cats and dogs can be
Friendly fireside companions
Or slash-lashing foes.

No Glorious Summer   *(one for the Shakespeare buffs!)*

Now is the winter
Of our discontent made sure -
By low cloud in York.

Wrong Tank

They burn lead-free fuel -
As they race through the village
Tanked up from the pub.

Here's a Double Dactyl "for the road".

Wrong Fuel

Stuck on the motorway,
"Bother", I'm heard to say,
"I just put Diesel oil
Into my tank".

Lack of mobility,
Combustibility -
Call out the RAC -
Wally, first rank!

And finally, returning to the title of the book, keep your eyes and ears open as you go about your daily business, and listen for the glory of the English language.

One Fowl Swoop

I'm totally obliviated,
Thoroughly washed through,
At one fowl swoop I've burnt my coop,
So now what shall I do?

My choice of words was not well bread,
A fare mistake to make,
A good mute point, a real damp squid,
And not a slice of cake.

If you've got this far, you're either a dedicated masochist or a cheat. Whichever, I hope you've enjoyed it! It only remains for me to say ...

Signing Off

Who am I?

I'm a husband, I'm a brother,
I'm a father with a mother,
I'm from south of Watford gap
Where there's Benskins draught on tap;
I'm a scientist by training,
Though not much of it's remaining,
So I've come to be a tutor
In the ways of the computer;
I write pantomimes and sketches
And perform them to the wretches
Who still seem to turn up read'ly
At the Theatre Club in Headley;
I'm a householder in Hants,
I write tracts on flying ants,
I'm a winner, I'm a loser,
I'm alive!

But my passport still says I'm a Systems Manager.

Index of Titles

About the author:

Jo Smith has lived in Headley near Bordon in Hampshire
for the past 14 years. During that time he has been
involved with local amateur dramatics and other village
activities while working as a computer consultant.

He has written pantomimes, plays, sketches and verses,
usually with a local flavour.

Other titles published by Owen Smith include:

Pantomimes and Plays:

❖   Cinderella, Jack and the Beanstalk, Puss in Boots,
    Robin Hood

❖   Marzipal, The Hindsight Saga

Compilations:

❖   Handle or Straight?, Soft Sunday,
    Wey Round Headley

£2.50   ISBN 1-873855-03-6